F*CK THAT SH*T

The 33 Things I Hate About Life

(A Swearing Coloring Book)

JANE WINDS

This page intentionally left blank.

ABOUT THE BOOK

If you want to go ahead and blow off some steam, then this is your book. Tired of obnoxious siblings? Frustrated with shitty drivers? Infuriated by the bullshit politicians? This is your book. Blow off some steam with this collection of 33 things that piss everyone off about life.

CONTENTS

This page intentionally left blank.

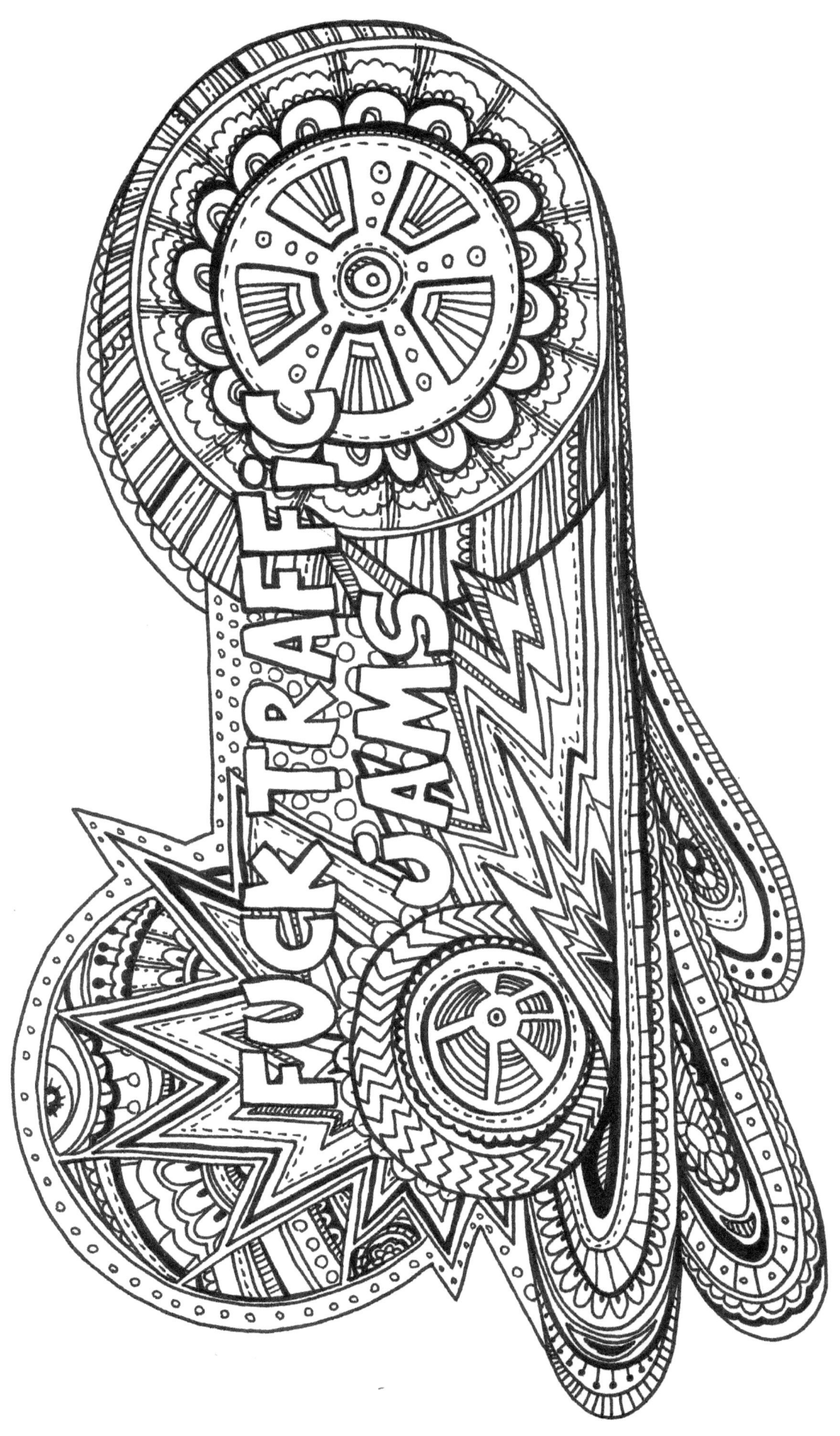

Plate 1.

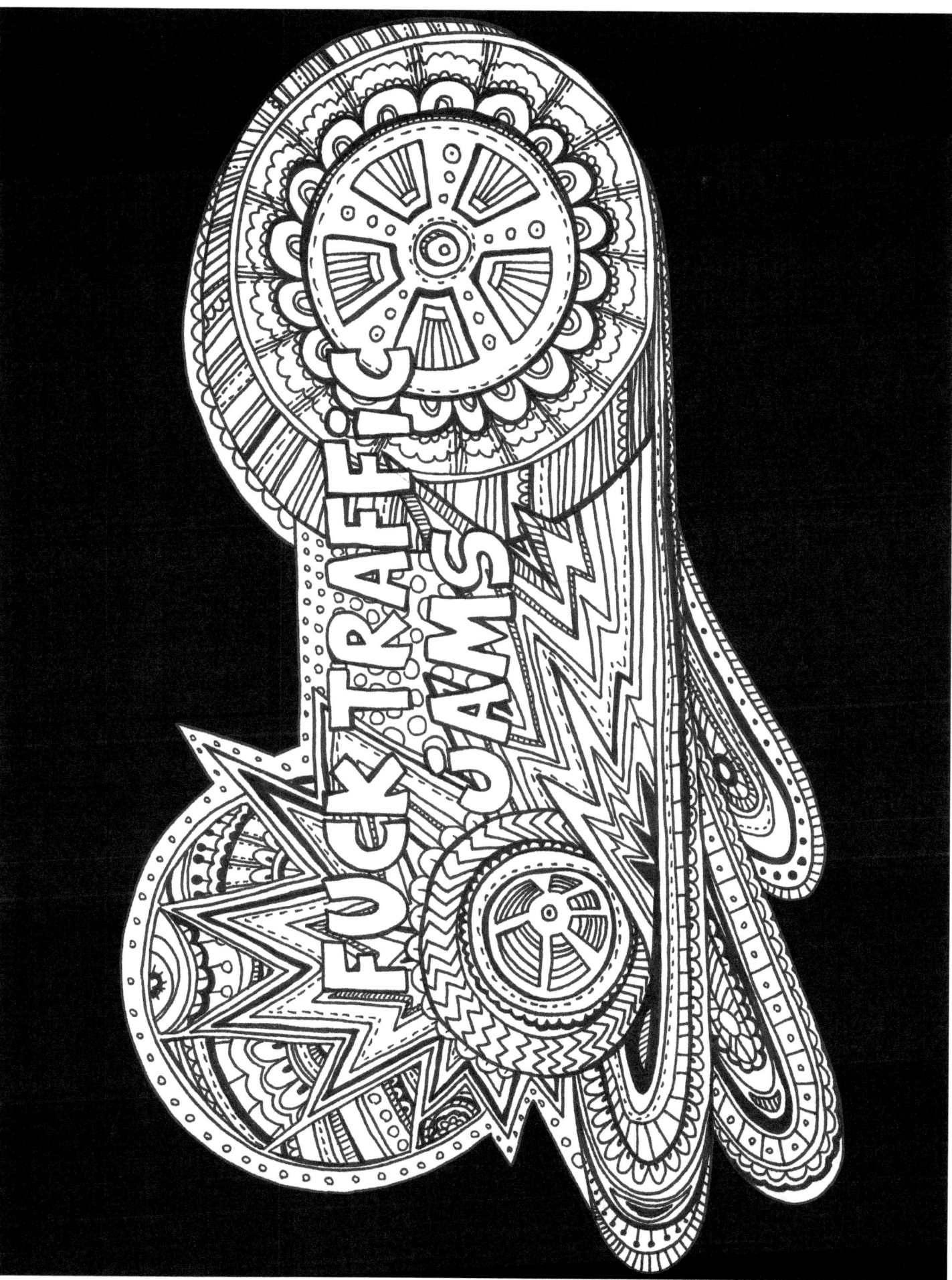

Plate 2.

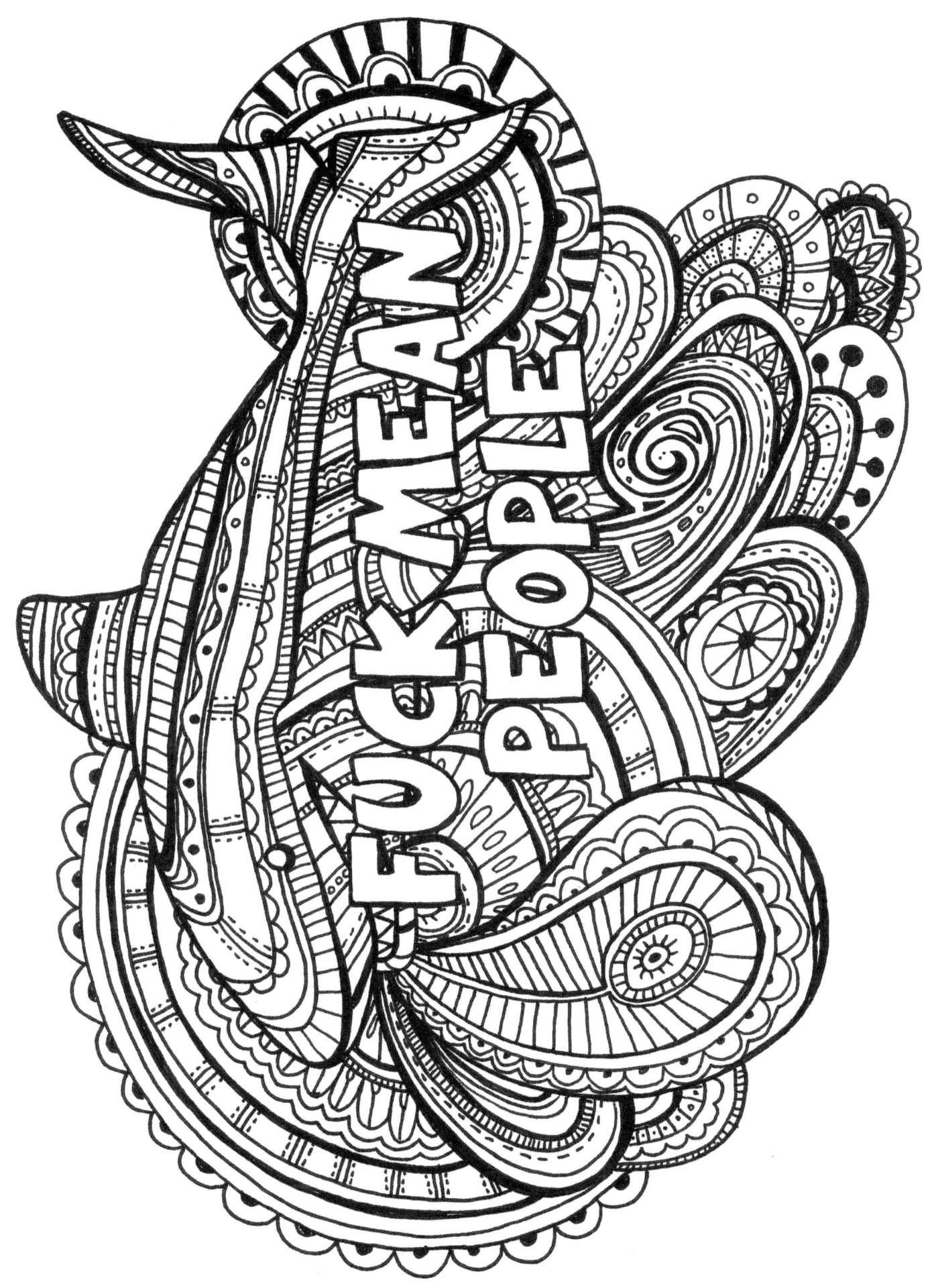

Plate 3.

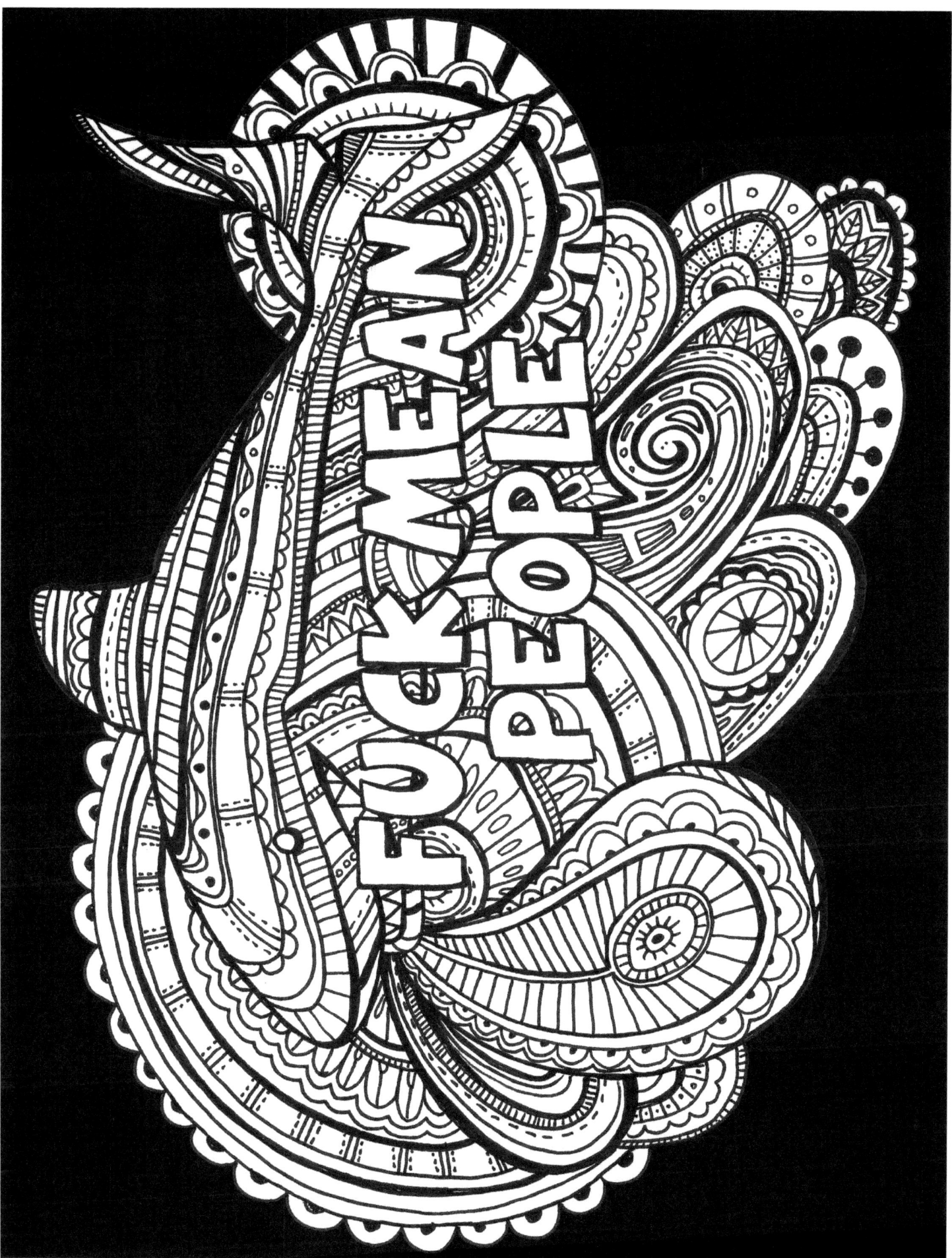

Plate 4.

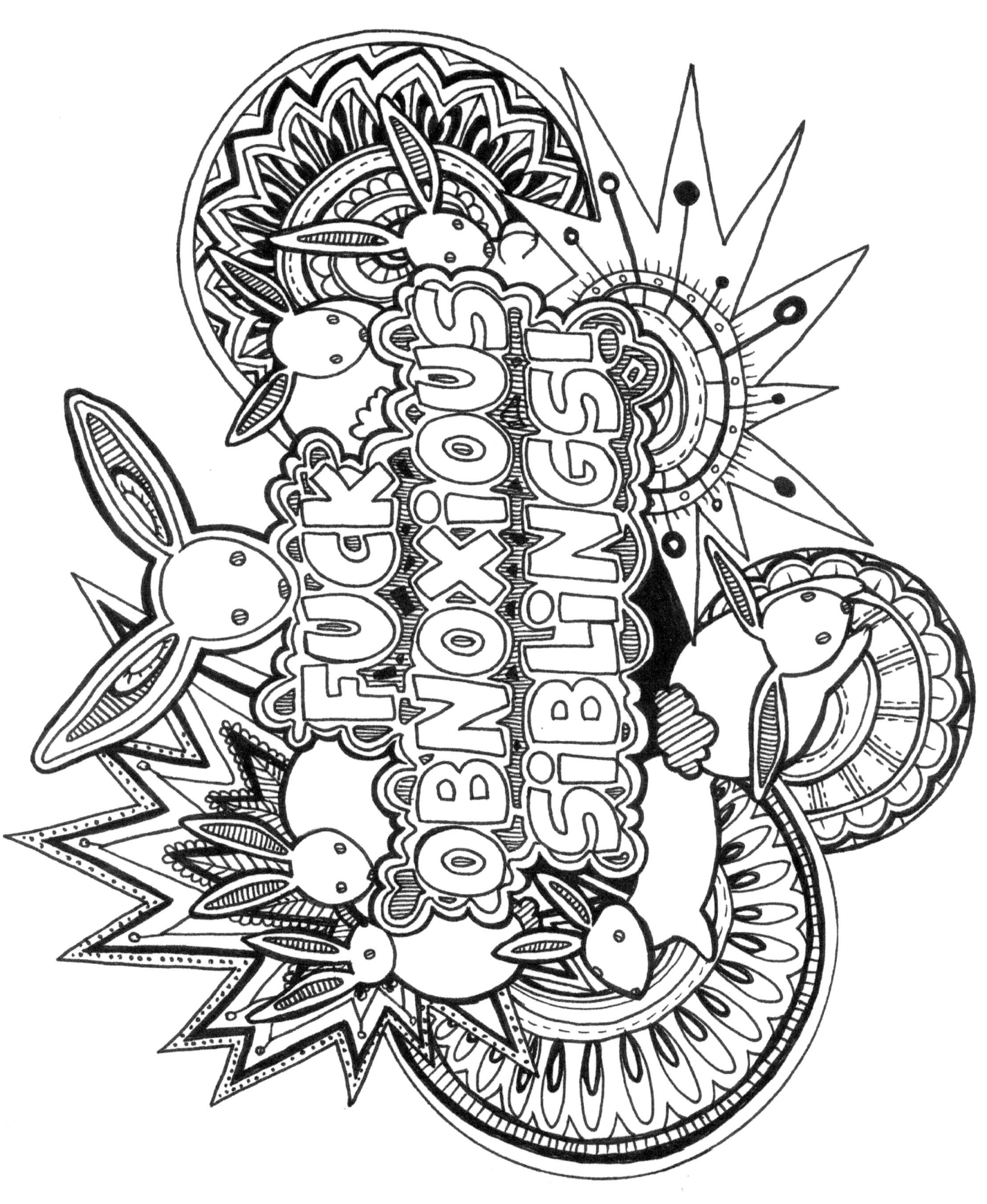

Plate 5.

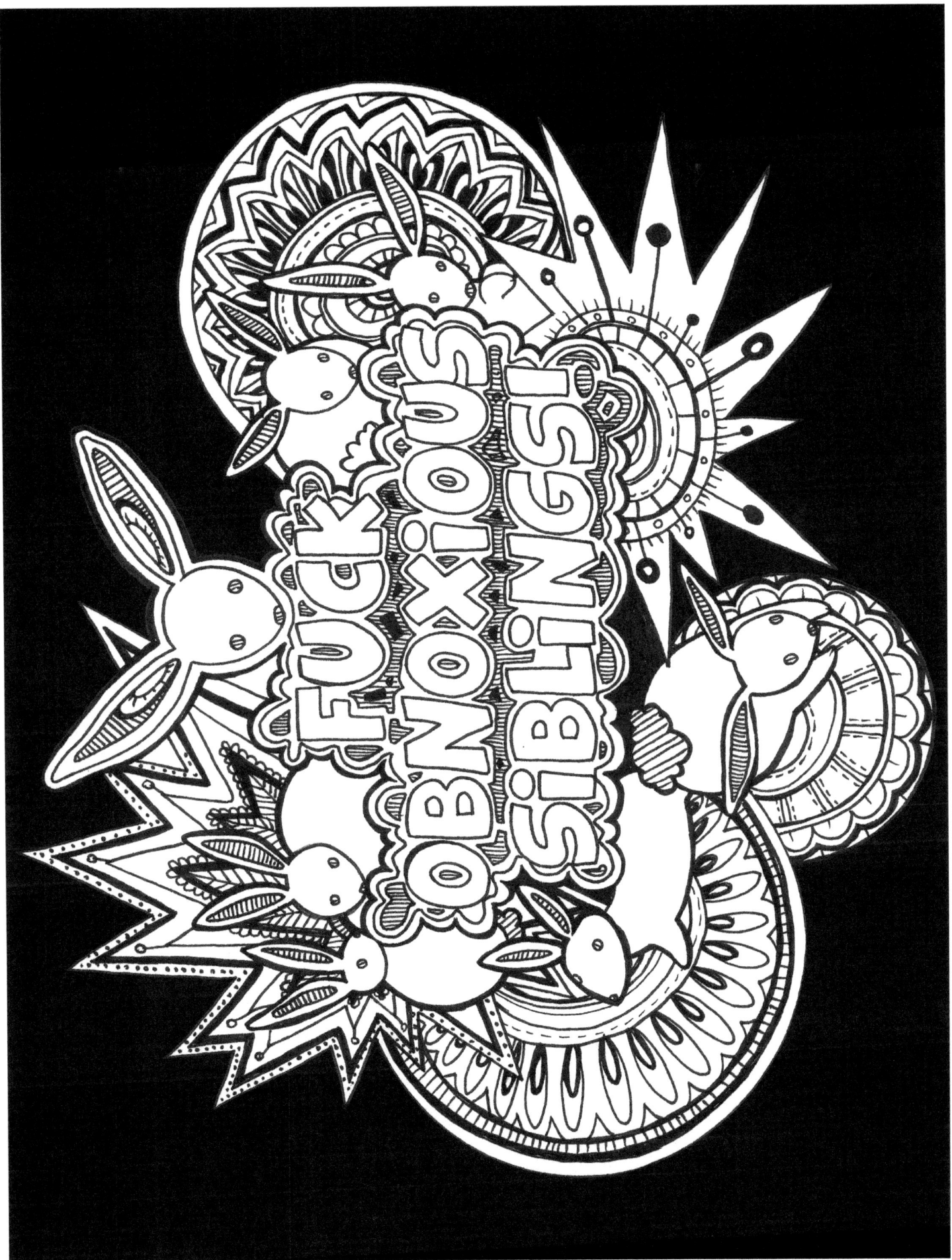

Plate 6.

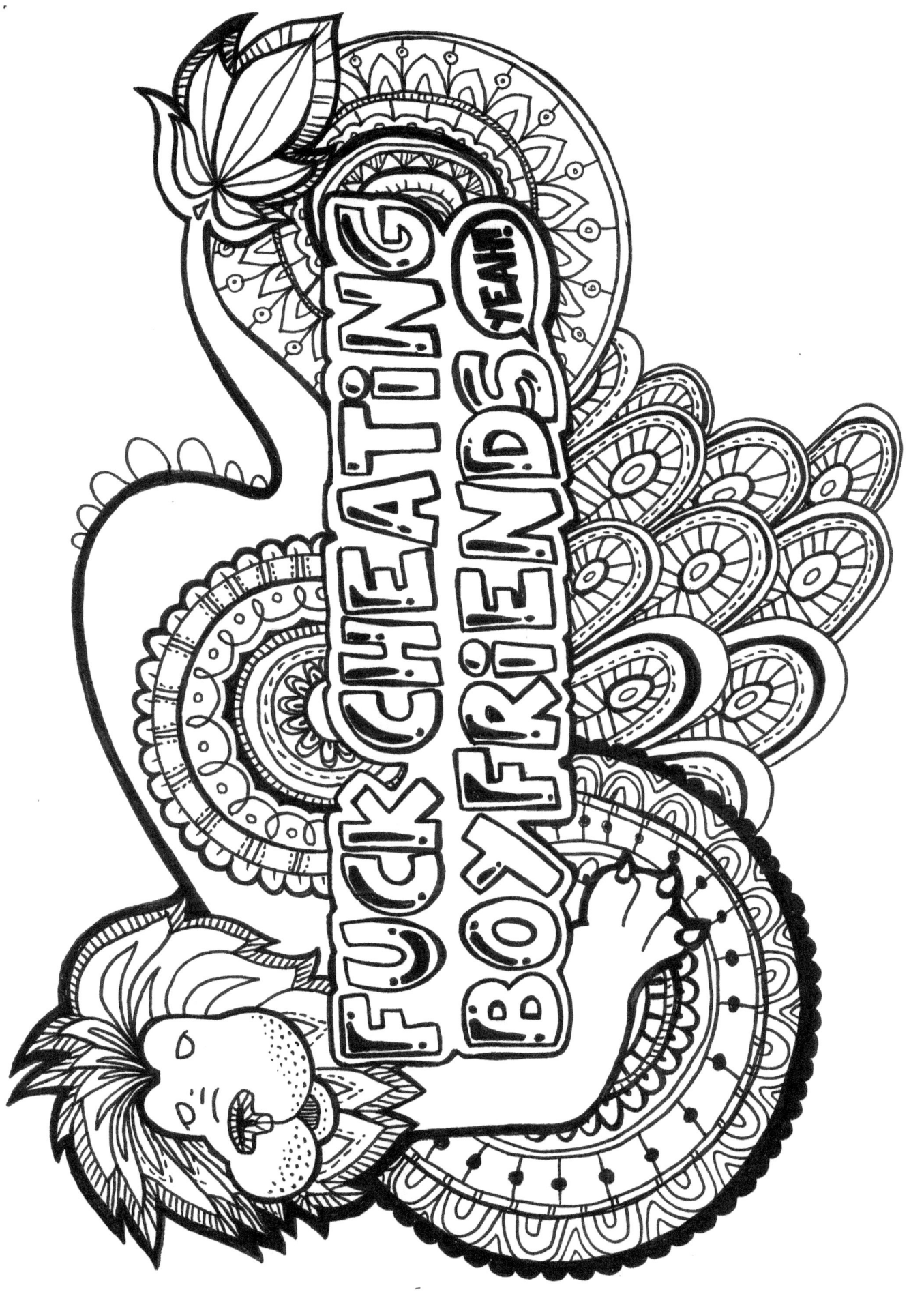

Plate 7.

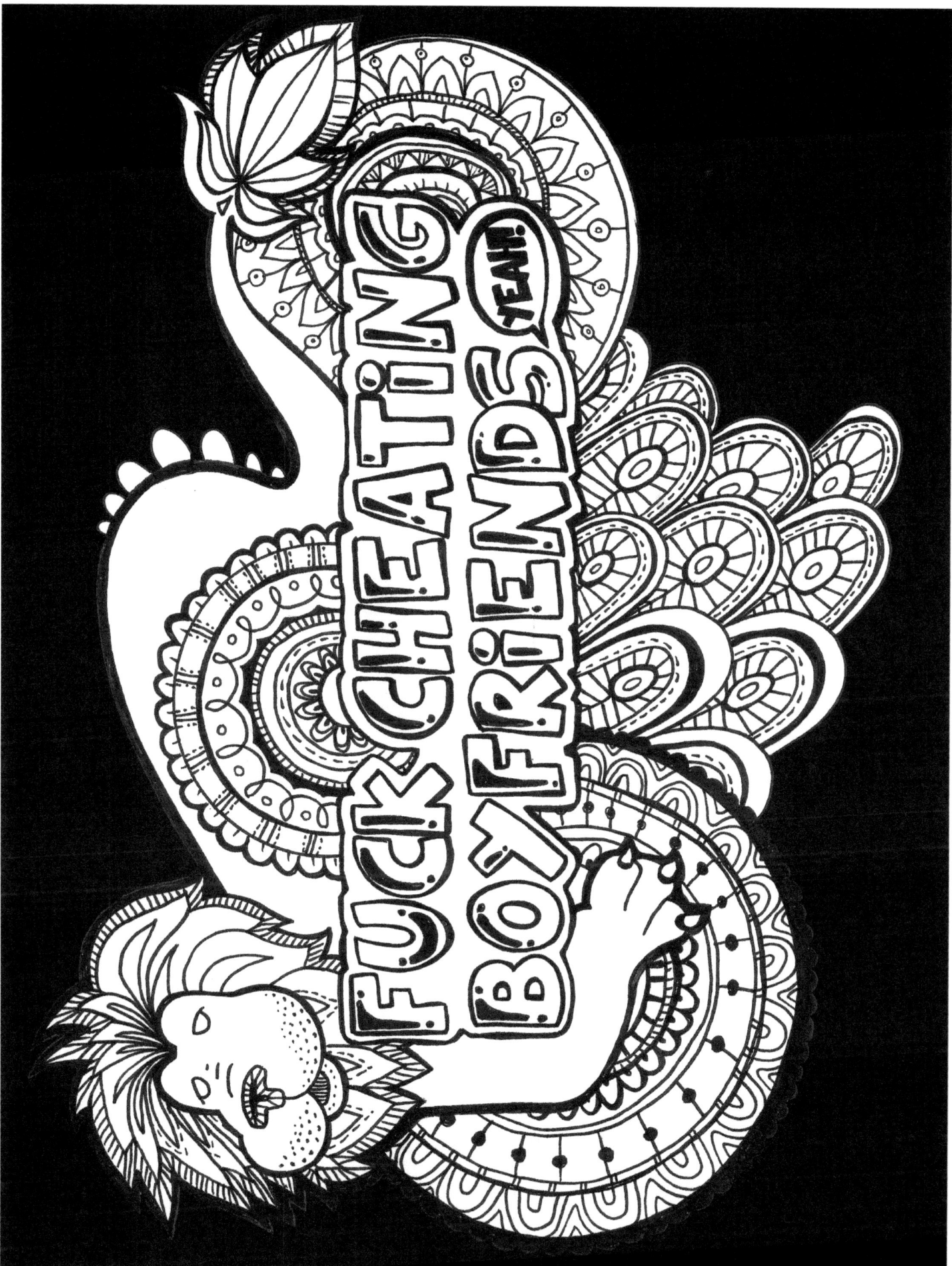

Plate 8.

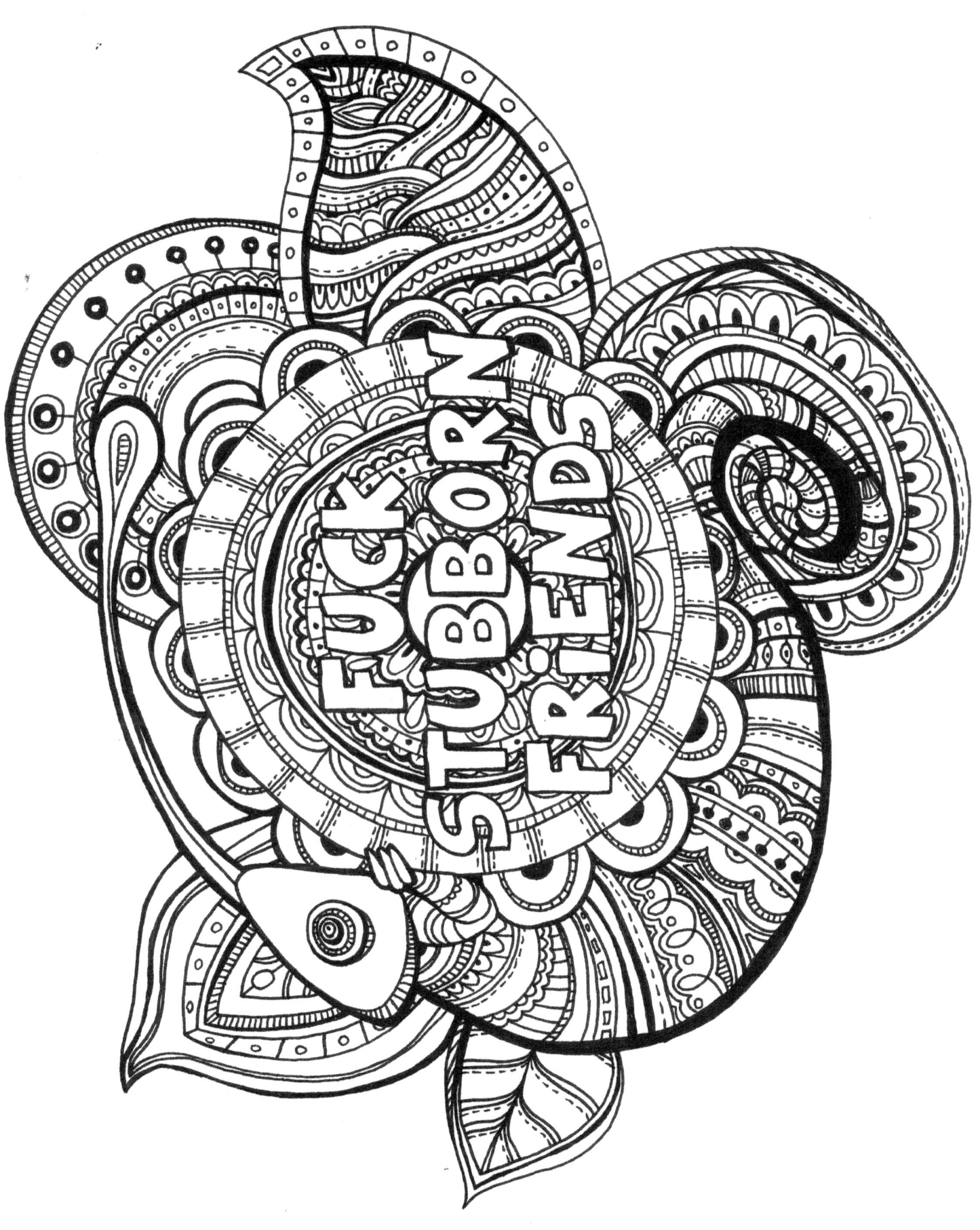

Plate 9.

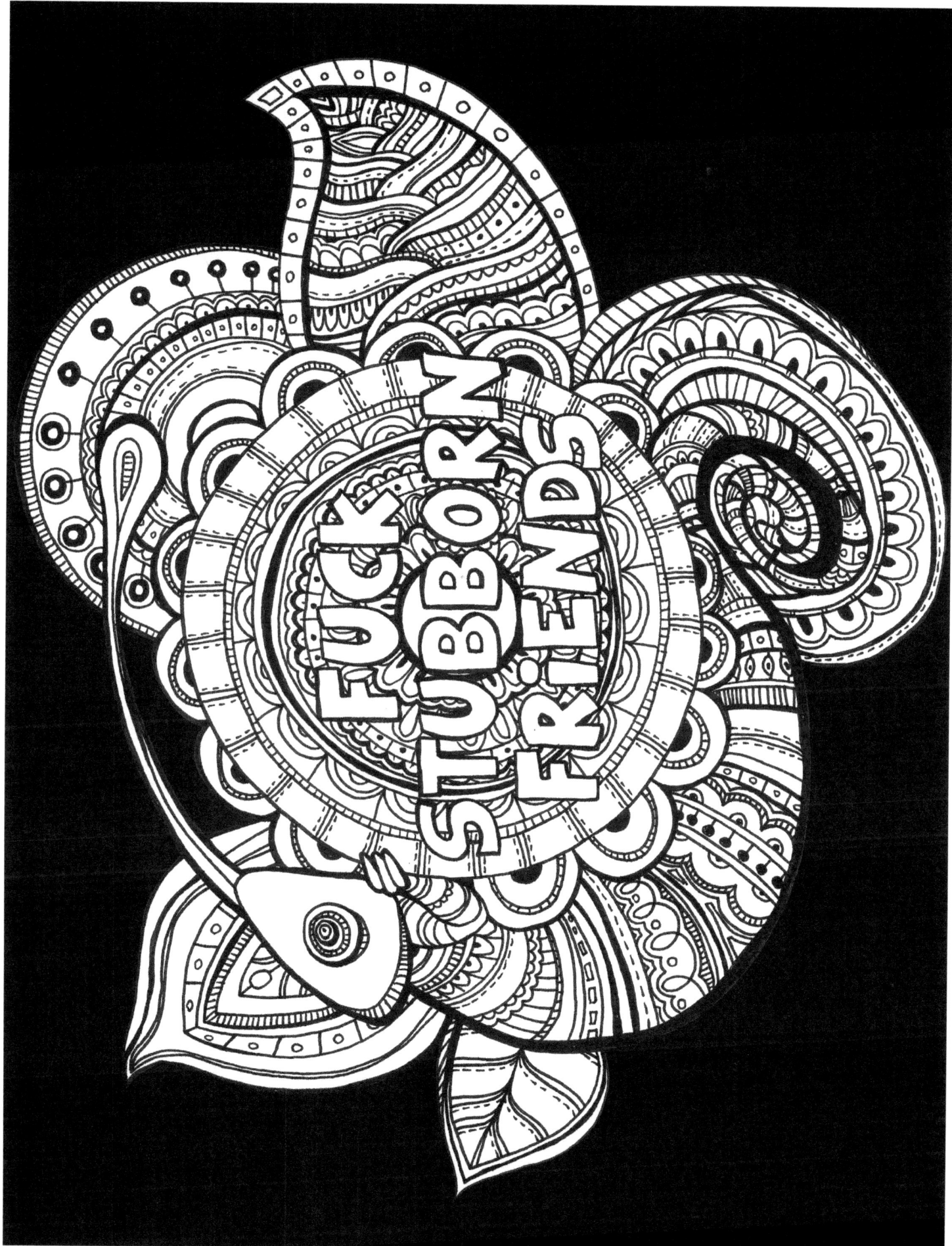

Plate 10.

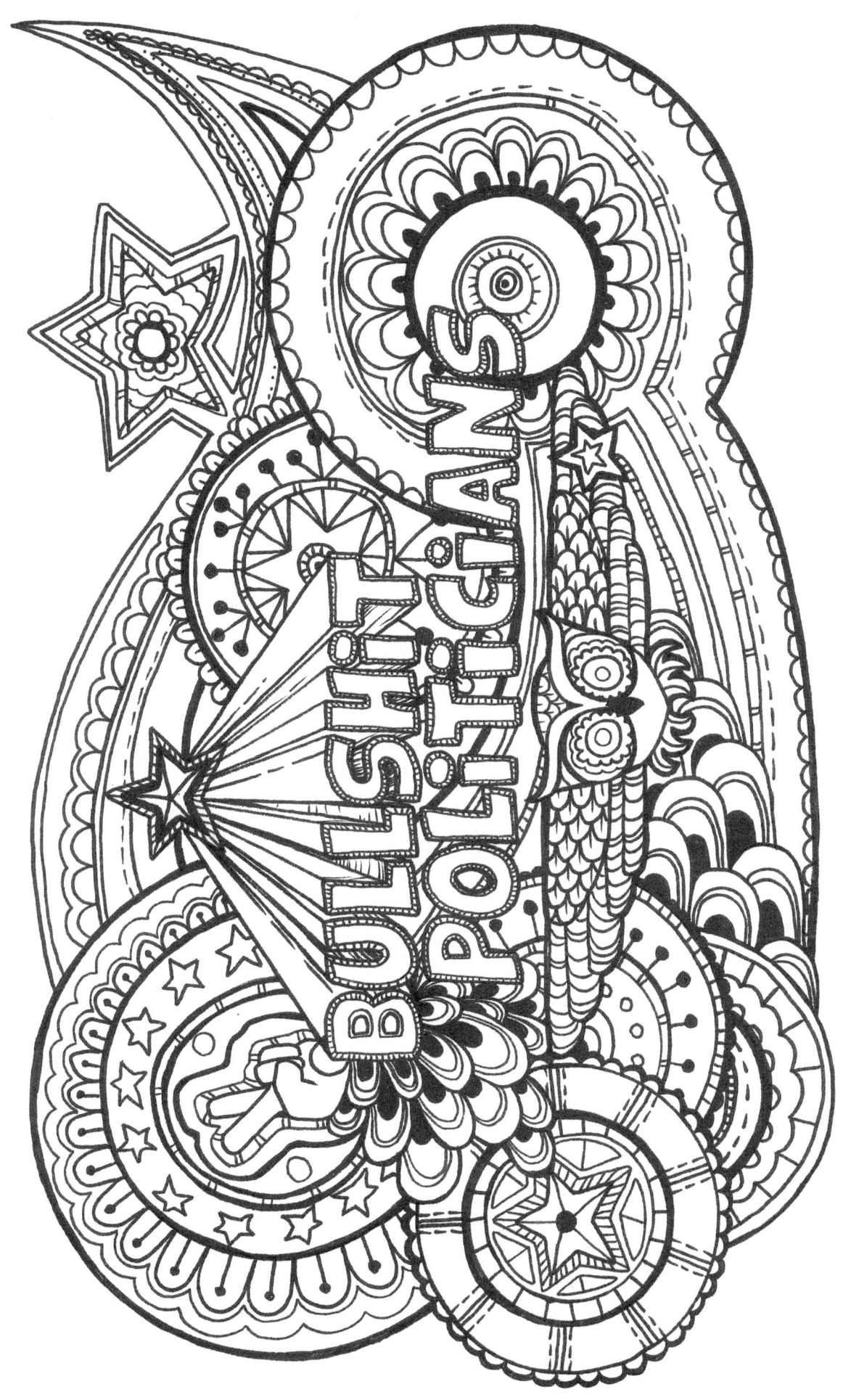

23

Plate 11.

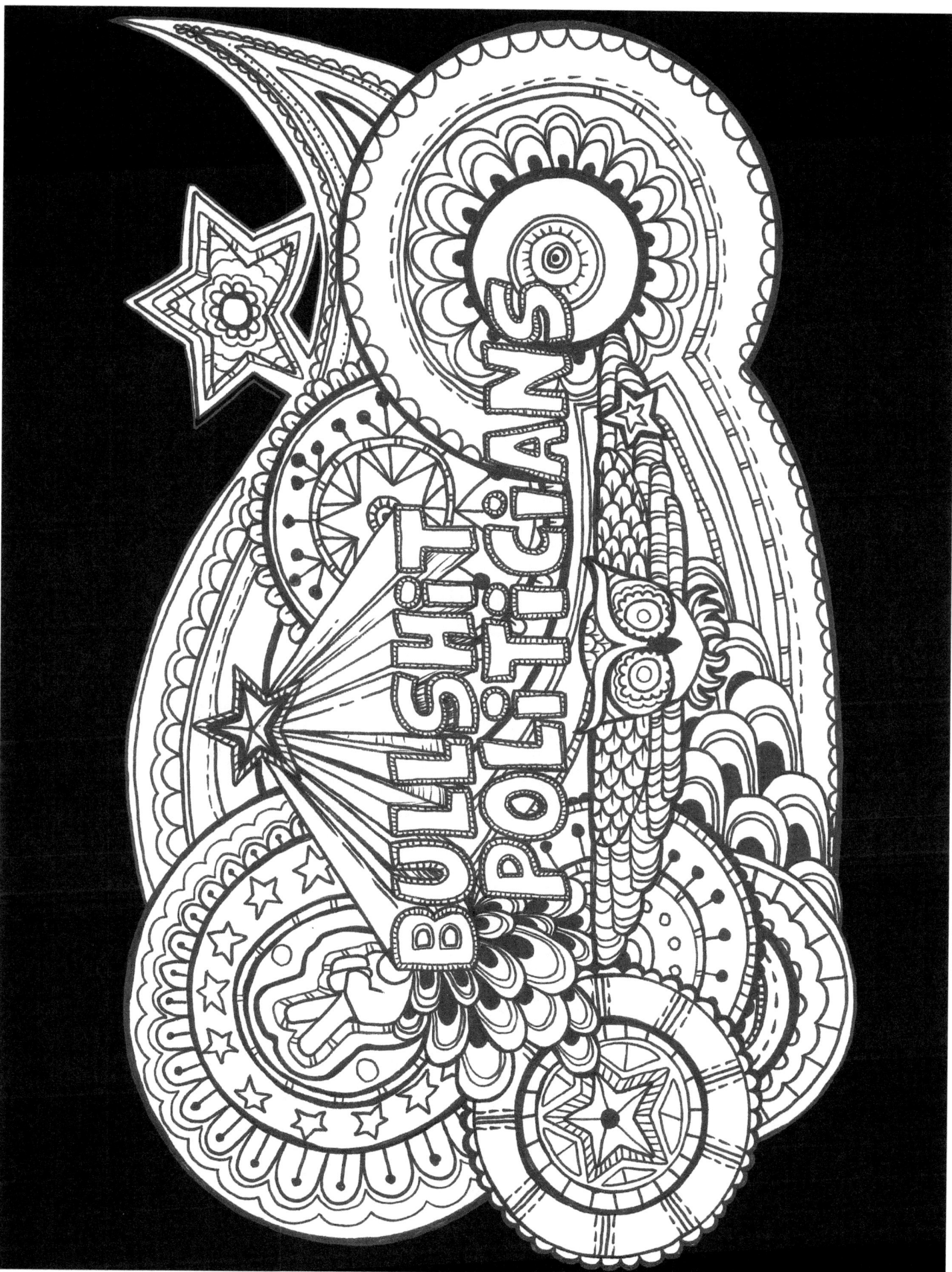

Plate 12.

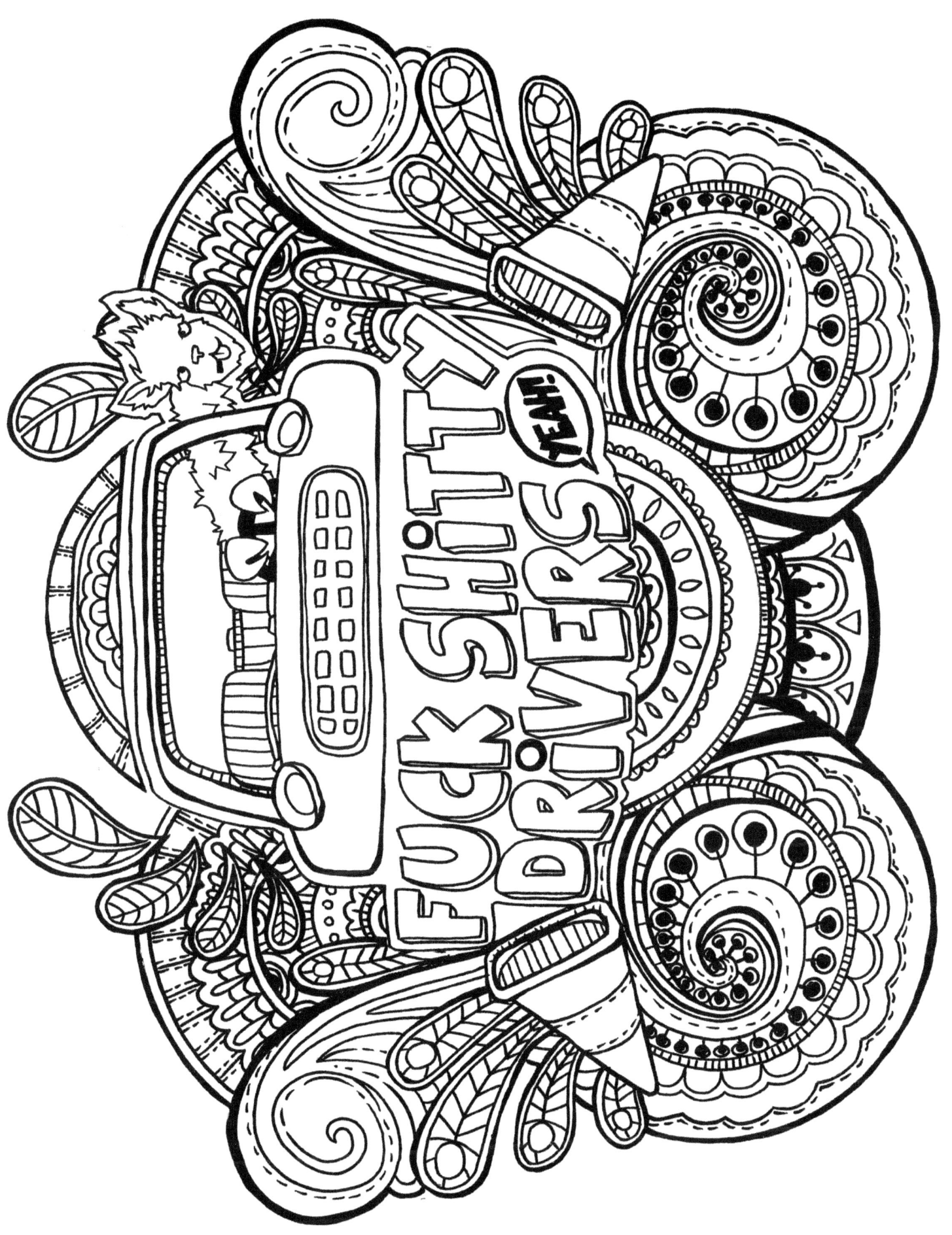

Plate 13.

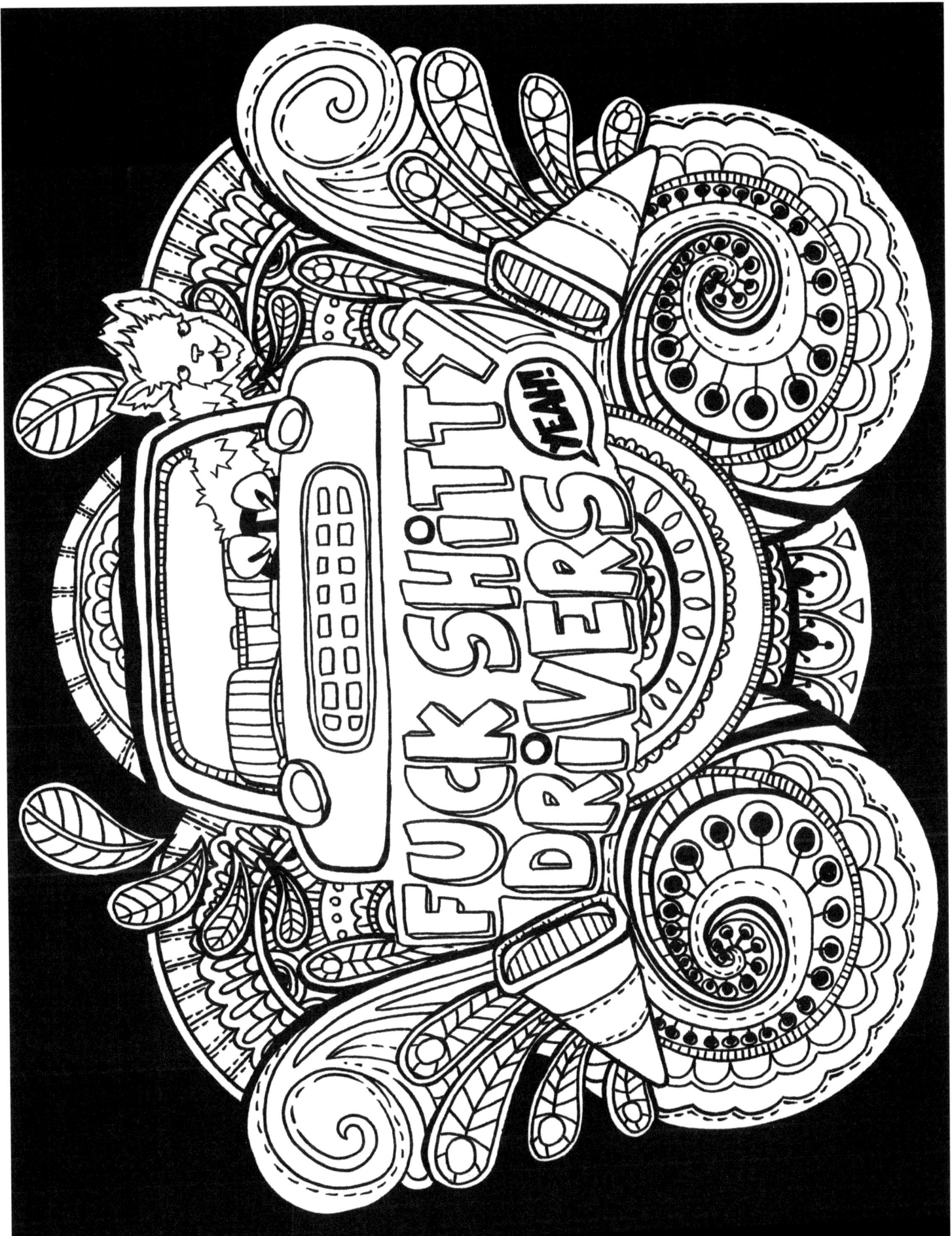

Plate 14.

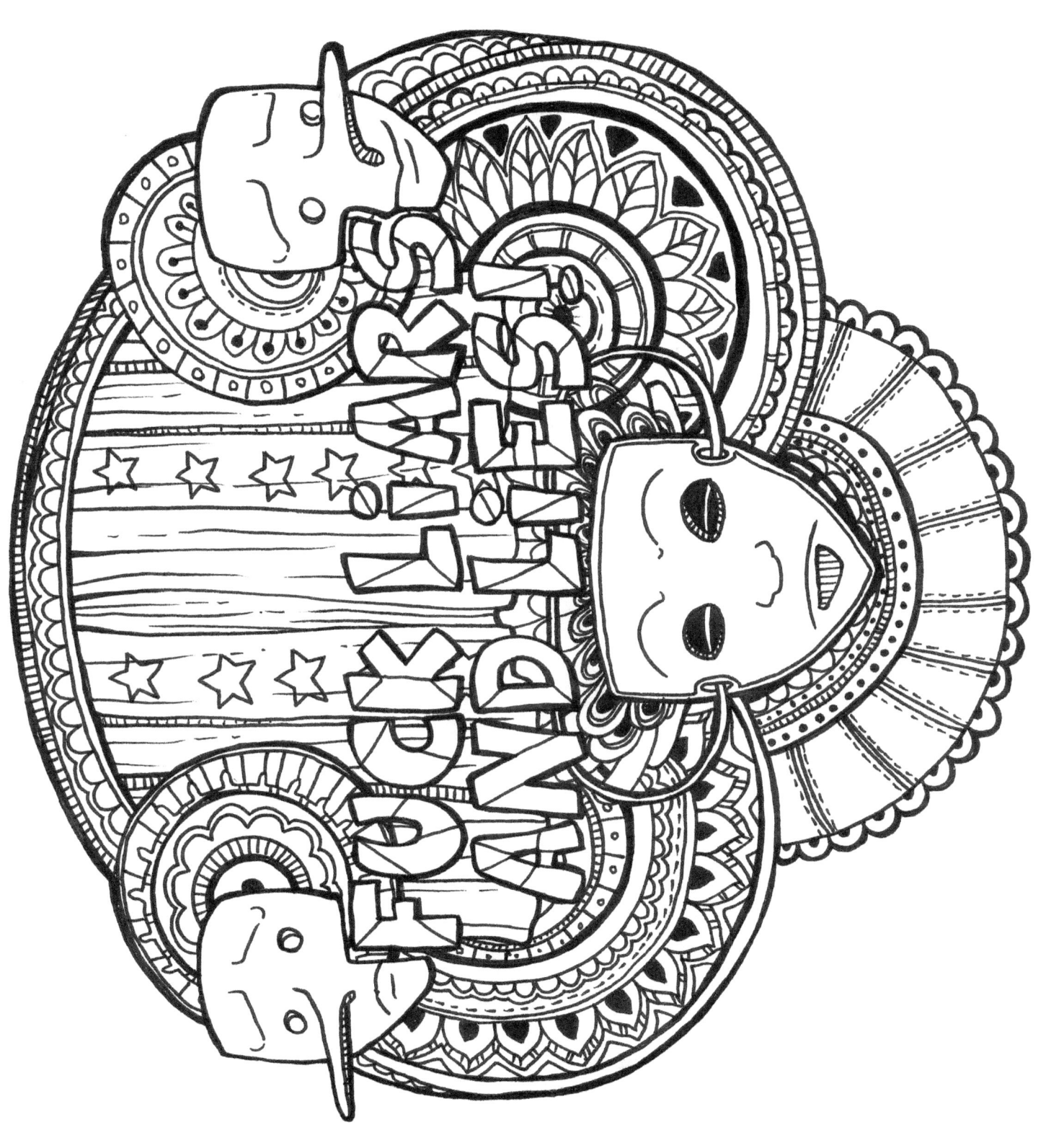

Plate 15.

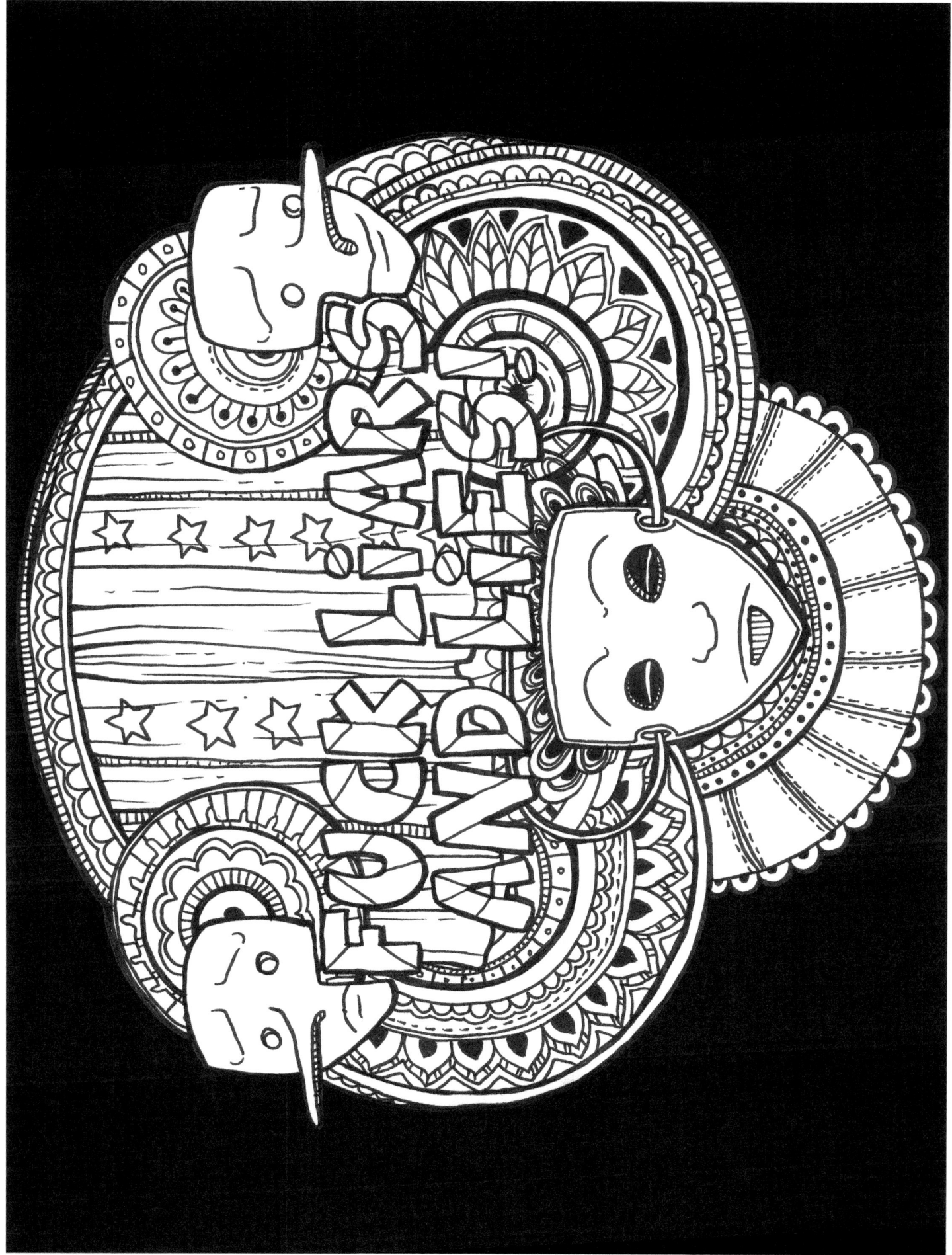

Plate 16.

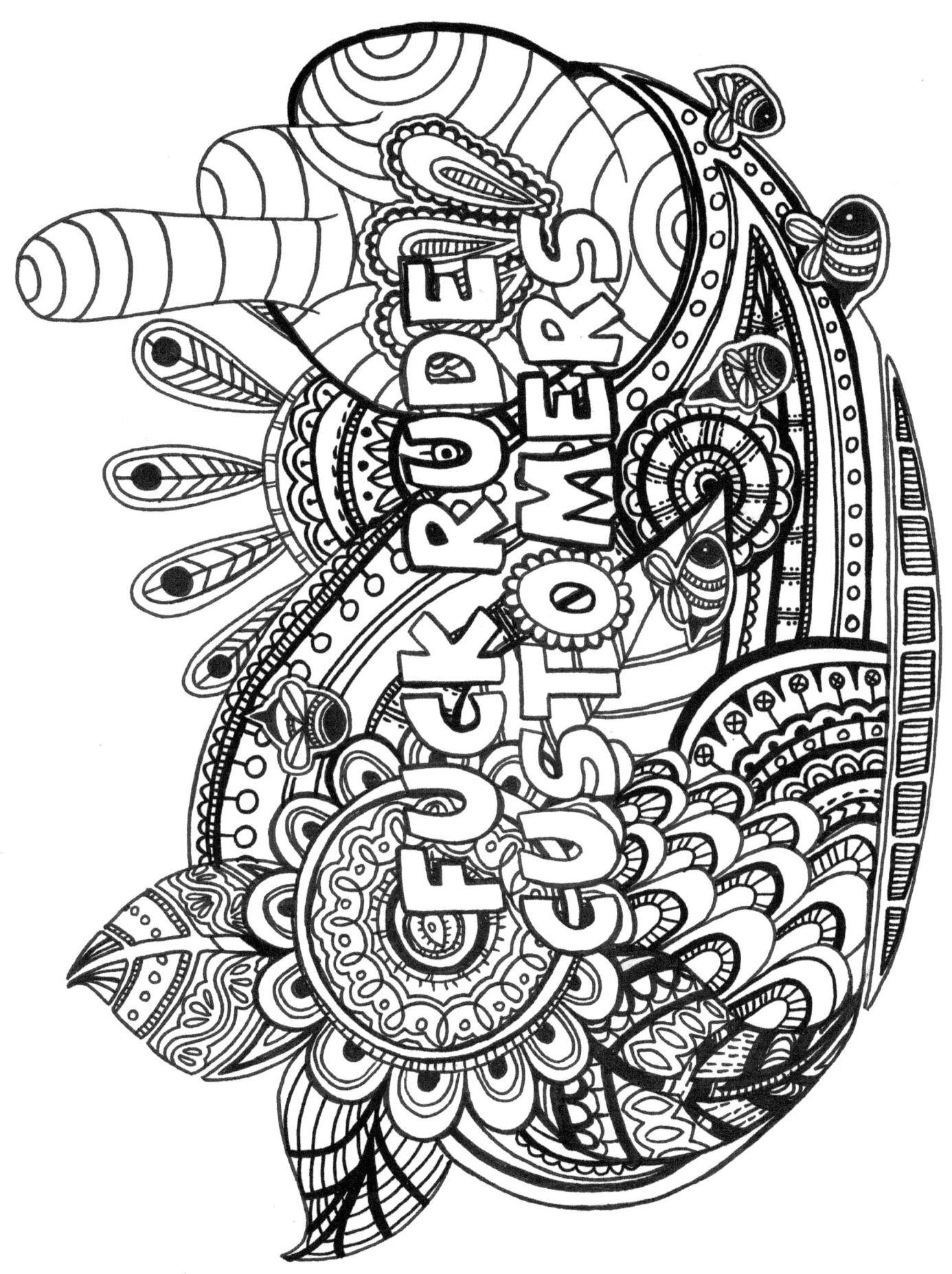

Plate 17.

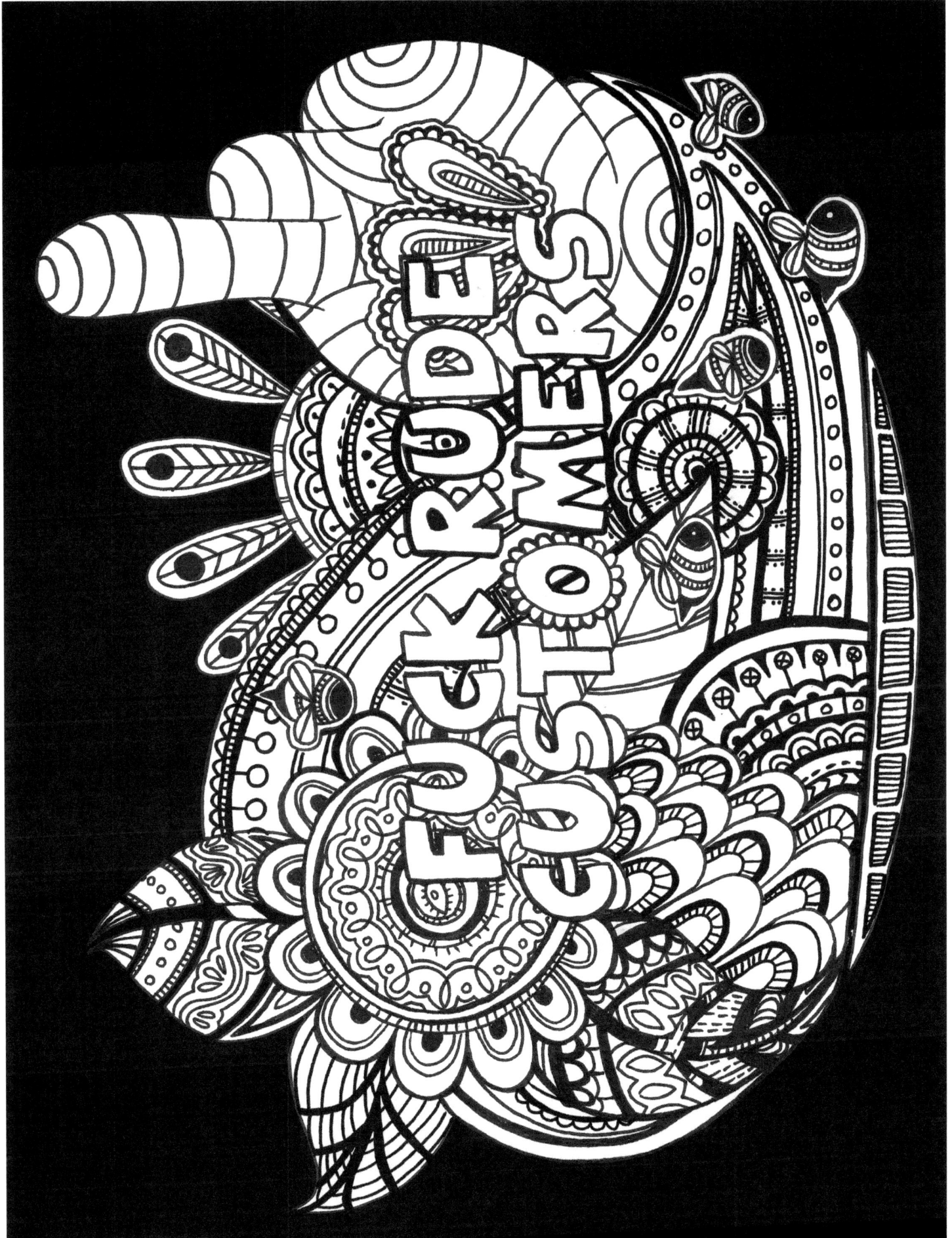

Plate 18.

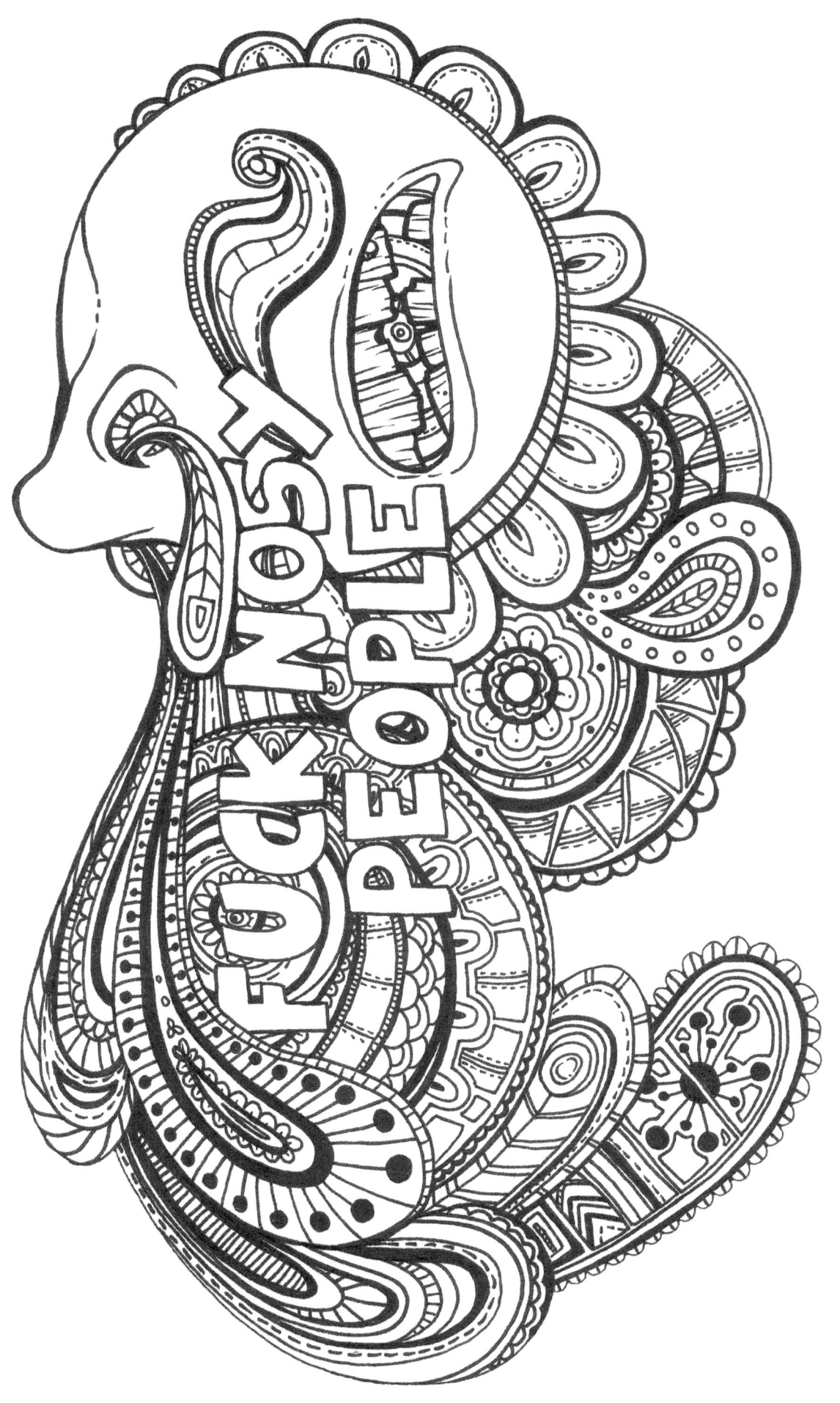

Plate 19.

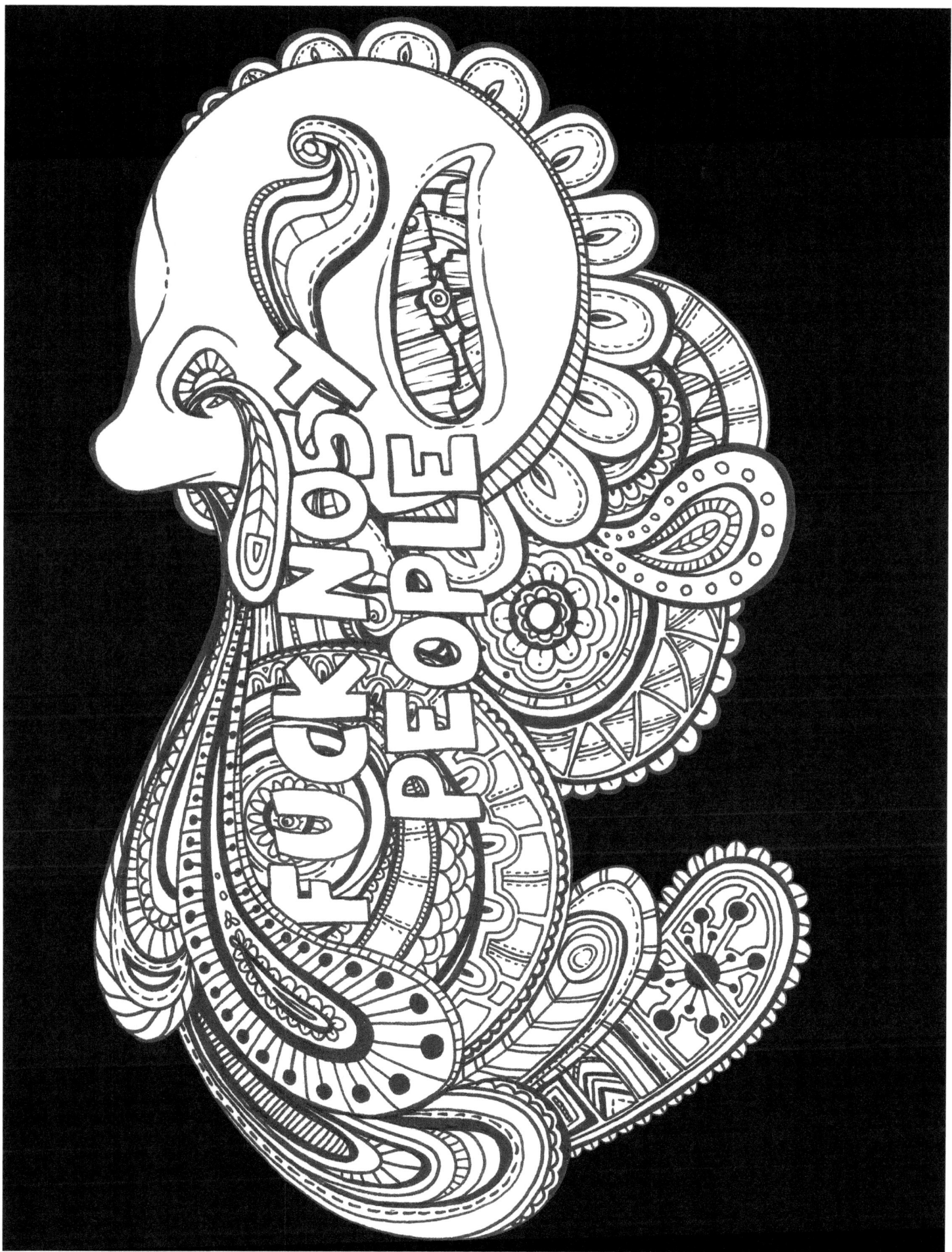

Plate 20.

This page intentionally left blank.

ABOUT THE BOOK

If you want to go ahead and blow off some steam, then this is your book. Tired of obnoxious siblings? Frustrated with shitty drivers? Infuriated by the bullshit politicians? This is your book. Blow off some steam with this collection of 33 things that piss everyone off about life.